S0-CFM-272

Book 24—Stories

Believing the Truth

Written by Anne de Graaf

Illustrated by José Pérez Montero

Family Time Bible Stories

Standard Publishing

Stories—Believing the Truth

Luke 15—20; Matthew 19—22, 26; Mark 10—12, 14; John 12

About Book 24

During Jesus last few weeks on earth, He performs more miracles and tells more stories than ever before.

Some of the stories Jesus tells are aimed at His enemies, the religious leaders who want Him silenced. These leaders were supposed to take care of the Jewish people. But over the years they had twisted God's love into a thousand tiny rules, making a heavy burden for the people.

Jesus has the good news of God's forgiveness. He gives the people a picture of His kingdom. Jesus' parables are special stories that amaze the people. His lessons on prayer, love, and forgiveness are preached with power and authority.

When asked who will come first in the kingdom of heaven, Jesus calls a little child to His side. Those who become like little children will come first. Jesus cares about families. When He teaches about not being proud and having simple trust, He is showing us a way to live joyfully every day.

Here begins Jesus' last week on earth. Time is running out. Who will believe the truth?

LIVING THE RIGHT LIFE

The Runaway

Luke 15:11-19

Jesus was surrounded by tax collectors and others that the religious leaders called sinners. Those leaders grumbled, "This man welcomes bad people as friends."

But Jesus told them a story about the love of God.

"There once was a man who had two sons. One day, the youngest son said, 'Father, give me the money that would be mine when you die.' The father agreed, and a few days later, the younger son left home.

"He went a long way, to a faraway country. There he spent all his money. Then a famine hit that land, which means there was very little food to eat.

"This younger son went to work on a farm, feeding pigs. All day long he watched the pigs eat and sighed, 'If only I could eat this food.'

"Before long, this son thought to himself, 'All of my father's workers have more than enough bread! Why am I here, starving? I should go back home. Yes, I'll go home and say to my father, "I've been wrong and I'm sorry. Please, don't even call me your son anymore, but hire me as a worker."'

"So the younger son left the pigs and traveled all the way home."

Coming Home

Luke 15:20-32

As Jesus told the story about the runaway son, He looked at the faces of the proud men around Him. These religious leaders had no patience with people who did not measure up.

"The father had been watching for

his son every day since he left from home. While the son was still a long way off, his father saw him. 'It's him!' the father shouted. 'My son has come home!' He ran and hugged his son, holding him tight and kissing him.

"But the son hung his head in shame. 'Father, I have done great wrong. Please, don't call me your son.'

"But the father paid no attention. He said to his slaves, 'Quickly, bring out the best robe and put it on him. Put a ring on his hand and get him some proper shoes. Kill the calf we were saving for a feast! Let's have a party! My son was dead, and now he lives. He was lost and has been found!' Before long, there was a great feast, going on, with music and dancing.

"The older son came home from working in the fields and asked a servant why there was a party. When he heard the reason, he became angry. His father tried to explain. But when he said, 'Please join us,' the older son turned away.

"'For years I have been the perfect son, working hard for you. Yet you never gave me a goat so I could have a party with my friends. But when this other son throws away his money, you give him everything.'

"'My son,' the father said. 'Everything I have belongs to you. Don't you see? This brother of yours was dead and now he's alive. He was lost and now has been found!'"

Money Lovers

Luke 16:10-14

The Pharisees may have heard Jesus, but they did not listen very well. They did not want to know about love and forgiveness. They only cared about their money and power.

Jesus said, "You can't worship money and God. It's like trying to serve two masters. You'll hate one master and love the other.

"You can know a lot about a person by the way he handles money. If someone can be trusted to use a little money wisely, he can be trusted with much more. And he can be trusted to handle more important things.

"A greedy person is ruled by the need for more money. God watches to see how people use the gifts He has given them."

Jesus showed the Pharisees they must choose between their love of money and the love of God. Which should come first?

The Rich Man and Lazarus

Luke 16:19-31

This is a story Jesus told so people would know they must make a choice, either for or against God.

"There once were two men. One was very rich, and the other was a beggar named Lazarus. Lazarus was covered with red sores. He lay in front of the rich man's gate, begging for crumbs left over from the rich man's meals. But the rich man paid no attention to poor and needy people like Lazarus.

"When Lazarus died, the angels came and carried him to Abraham's side. There he felt no more pain and he never felt hungry.

"The rich man also died and was buried. He was sent to a place of suffering. From where he was, the rich man could look up and see Lazarus.

"'Father Abraham!' the rich man called out. 'Send Lazarus with just a little water so I can cool off my tongue! I'm so thirsty here!'

"But Abraham said, 'Don't you remember how during your life you had so much and he had nothing? But now he has his good things. Besides, there's a huge hole between here and there. No one can cross over.'

"Then the rich man said, 'Send Lazarus to warn my five brothers so that they change their ways and do not have to come here!'

"'Ah, but they can read the warnings themselves. Moses and the prophets all call the people back to God,' Abraham said.

"'But Father Abraham,' the rich man called back. 'If someone goes to them from the dead, they'll be sure to listen!

"'If they don't listen to Moses and the prophets,' Abraham answered, 'they won't listen to someone from the dead.'"

CHOICES TO MAKE

How to Forgive

Luke 17:3-6

Suppose someone hurts you. Suppose later that person comes and says he is sorry. What would you do?

Jesus talked to His disciples about forgiving others. "If a man sins against you seven times a day, and returns to you seven times, saying each time, 'I am sorry,' then forgive him."

It was that simple. But the disciples said "Give us more faith!"

Jesus reminded them, "Even with faith as small as a mustard seed, you can tell a tree to pull up its roots and be planted in the sea, and it will obey you."

But how does a person get that much faith? How can anyone believe the impossible is possible? God is the answer. The only way to have the kind of faith which moves trees is to ask Jesus to give it to you. It comes from God, not from inside us. And it is a gift we must ask for.

Even with a little faith, you can forgive someone who has hurt you, then said he was sorry, seven times.

When Jesus Comes Back

Luke 17:20-36

Jesus taught often about the kingdom of God. Once, the Pharisees asked Him when the kingdom of God would come. "You cannot see God's kingdom," Jesus said, "because it is within people."

Then He told the disciples, "When I come back, it will be suddenly, without warning, just as lightning streaks across a night sky and no one knows where it will strike next.

"On that day it will be too late to change your mind. Whoever tries to save his life then shall lose it, and whoever is willing to give up everything will keep all that matters.

"On that night, where two people sleep, one will be taken and the other will be left behind. If there are two women grinding grain, one will be taken and the other will not."

Why? What is the difference between those who are taken to Heaven and those who are left behind? The difference is whether they chose to believe in Jesus and live His way.

Lessons About Prayer

Luke 18:1-8

Sometimes God's answer to our prayers is "Wait." It can be hard to keep on praying during those times, but that is exactly what we should do. Jesus told a story to His disciples so that they, and we, would not lose heart.

"There once was a judge who was not afraid of anyone. One day a widow came to him, asking for protection. She was helpless, so again and again she begged this judge to help her.

"In the end he agreed. But do you know why? He didn't help the widow because he knew it would please God. And he didn't do it because he cared about what other people thought. He helped her because she had kept on asking, over and over and over again.

"Listen," Jesus said. "God wants what is right for His chosen people, but they must also believe in Him. When they cry out to Him day and night, believing He can help, He won't wait long to answer their prayers."

"But I wonder," Jesus said, "will the Son of Man find anyone with faith like this?"

JESUS AND FAMILIES

Why Is There Divorce?

Matthew 19:3-11; Mark 10:2-9

Sometimes it happens that a husband and wife break up their marriage. This is what divorce means. It is a very sad time for everybody in the family. Everyone feels hurt. Often children feel the most hurt, though.

When a mother or father moves out of the home, many children feel like it is their fault. But it isn't. They shouldn't blame themselves. It happens sometimes that mothers and fathers choose not to live together. There can be many reasons for this happening, but the children are never to blame.

Some Pharisees came to Jesus to try to trick Him. "Can a man divorce his wife for any reason at all?" they asked.

Jesus said that God was the one who brings men and women together in marriage. God does not want husbands and wives to separate what He has joined together.

Then the Pharisees said, "Then why did Moses say it was all right to divorce?" The Pharisees wanted to trap Jesus into saying something that went against the law God had given to Moses.

But Jesus said, "Because of your hard and stubborn hearts, you were allowed to leave your wives! But that is not how it was from the beginning."

When Jesus' disciples heard this, they said, "But if that's the way it is, then it must be better not to marry at all!"

Jesus said, "Not everyone needs to get married. Some people can serve God best if they do not marry."

"Let the Children Come to Me"

Matthew 19:13-14; Mark 10:13-16; Luke 18:15-17

One day a group of mothers brought their babies to Him, asking if He would bless them.

But the disciples said, "Go away and leave the Teacher alone!"

Jesus was upset. "No!" He said, "Don't send these children away. Let them come to me."

He looked at His disciples and used the children to teach them more about His kingdom. "The kingdom of Heaven belongs to anyone who is as trusting and willing to believe as these little ones. Anyone who won't receive the kingdom of God like a little child will never enter it."

Then Jesus took the children in his arms, touched their heads and blessed them. Mothers smiled as the children came running back into their arms. And the disciples looked on, smiling, even though at first they had been angry at the children.

THE FIRST AND THE LAST
The Rich Young Man

Matthew 19:16-23; Mark 10:17-23; Luke 18:18-23

After Jesus blessed the children, a man ran up to Him and knelt in the dust. "Good Teacher, what must I do in order to live forever?" he asked.

"If you want to live, follow the commandments," Jesus said.

But the man said, "I have been careful to follow all the commandments since I was a boy."

Jesus knew there was one thing that stood between this young man and God. The young man loved God, but he loved being rich even more. So Jesus said, "Go, sell your things and give your money to the poor, and you will have treasure in Heaven. Then come, follow me."

But when the young man heard this, he turned away. He knew deep down that he had not given God first place in his life. He was not willing to give up his riches and follow Jesus. So he walked away very, very sad.

Jesus looked around at His disciples. "Truly, it's a very, very hard thing for a rich man to enter Heaven."

Who Comes First?

Matthew 19:24-30; Mark 10:24-31; Luke 18:24-30

After the rich young man walked away, Jesus said, "It's easier for a camel to go through the eye of a needle than for a rich man to love God more than his money."

This astounded His disciples. "But who can be saved then, if not the rich?" they asked.

Jesus looked at them. "No one, if it were left up to men. But with God anything can happen."

Jesus is part of God's plan for saving people from all their wrongs. Through Jesus, and not because of how rich or good anyone might be, people can enter the kingdom of Heaven. But first they must follow Jesus and be willing to love Him more than anything else and especially more than money.

When Peter heard this, he wondered what the disciples might get in return for all they had given up. "We've left everything and followed you," he said.

Jesus answered, "Whenever anyone is willing to give up home or family when I ask it, he will receive a hundred times as much in the world to come. Many who are first here on earth will come last in Heaven, and those who are last will be first."

Vineyard Workers

Matthew 20:1-16

Jesus told His disciples this story.

"The kingdom of Heaven is like a man who owned some land. He hired some men early in the morning to work in his vineyard. A few hours later, he went out and hired more workers. He went out several more times and hired more workers. The last time, he saw some men with nothing to do and asked, 'Why have you been standing around all day?'

"They answered, 'No one hired us.'

"The landowner said, 'You go into the vineyard then, and work for me.'

When evening came, the landowner of the farm asked all his workers to line up so he could pay them.

"First the owner paid the group he had hired late in the day. Then he went to the others. But even though they had worked more hours, he gave them the very same amount.

"Those hired first grumbled, 'We thought we would get more. Those last men worked only one hour, but we sweated in the hot sun all day.'

"The owner said, 'Friends, you were paid the wage I promised you. If I choose to be generous with the others, are you envious?"

Jesus looked up at the puzzled faces of His disciples. "In this way the last will be first, and the first last."

Jesus Predicts His Death

Matthew 20:17-19; Mark 10:32-34; Luke 18:31-34

Jesus and the disciples were on their way to Jerusalem for the Passover feast. He took the twelve men He had chosen and called them away from the others.

"Listen to me," He said urgently. "When we arrive in Jerusalem, all the things that are written through the prophets about the Son of Man will happen. He will be betrayed to the religious leaders, and handed over to the non-Jews. They will make fun of Him, beat Him, and crucify Him. But on the third day He will rise again."

The twelve did not understand any of this, since the meaning was hidden from them. They were afraid. But as Jesus continued down the road, headed toward Jerusalem, there was nothing they could do but follow.

Jesus' words echoed in their ears: "They will mock Him and spit upon Him and hit Him and kill Him, and three days later He will rise again."

To Learn to Serve

Matthew 20:20-28; Mark 10:35-45

James and John asked Jesus to do them a favor.

"What do you want me to do for you?" Jesus asked.

"When You are in Your kingdom, let us be Your favorites. Give us places of honor next to Your throne. Let one of us sit on Your right side, and the other on Your left."

"But you have no idea what you are asking," Jesus said. It was as if they had not even heard His warning about the hard times looming ahead. All they could think about was how great they might become.

Jesus patiently tried to help His disciples see past their own selfishness. "Are you able to drink the cup that I drink?" Jesus wanted to know if they were willing to suffer as He would.

"Yes," James and John said.

"Then you will drink from that cup. But the places at my right and left in the kingdom of Heaven are not mine to give."

While Jesus was saying this, the other ten disciples had moved closer so they could listen. They were mad at James and John for asking Jesus for a share in His glory. Jesus looked up and saw their hurt faces. He felt the confusion and fear in their hearts. So He gathered them all around Him.

"You know how kings make others serve them? But this isn't how it will be for you. Whoever wants to be great in my kingdom must serve the rest of you. Whoever wishes to be first must be willing to come last."

ON THE WAY TO JERUSALEM

Healing Bartimaeus

Matthew 20:29-34; Mark 10:46-52; Luke 18:35-43

The crowd following Jesus to Jerusalem passed along the road to Jericho. There, a blind man named Bartimaeus sat begging.

When Bartimaeus heard that it was Jesus passing by, he called out as loud as he could. "Lord, have mercy on me, Son of David!"

"Hush!" the people around him said. "You there, be quiet! Stop making so much noise!"

But the blind man ignored all the people around him and kept right on yelling. "Help me! Lord, have mercy on me, Son of David!"

Jesus stopped. "Call him here," He said.

So the people around Bartimaeus gave him a hand up. "The Teacher is calling for you. Hurry and stand up."

Bartimaeus threw his cloak on the ground and let the people lead him to Jesus. Jesus said, "What do you want me to do for you?"

"Oh, Teacher, I want to see! said Bartimaeus.

"Go your way," Jesus said. "Your faith has healed you."

Suddenly, Bartimaeus could see! "Oh, Teacher, thank You," he whispered. The smile on Jesus' face grew wider. Jesus turned, then, to continue down the road. Bartimaeus followed.

He shouted, "I can see! Praise God! I can see!" And this time, no one told him to be quiet.

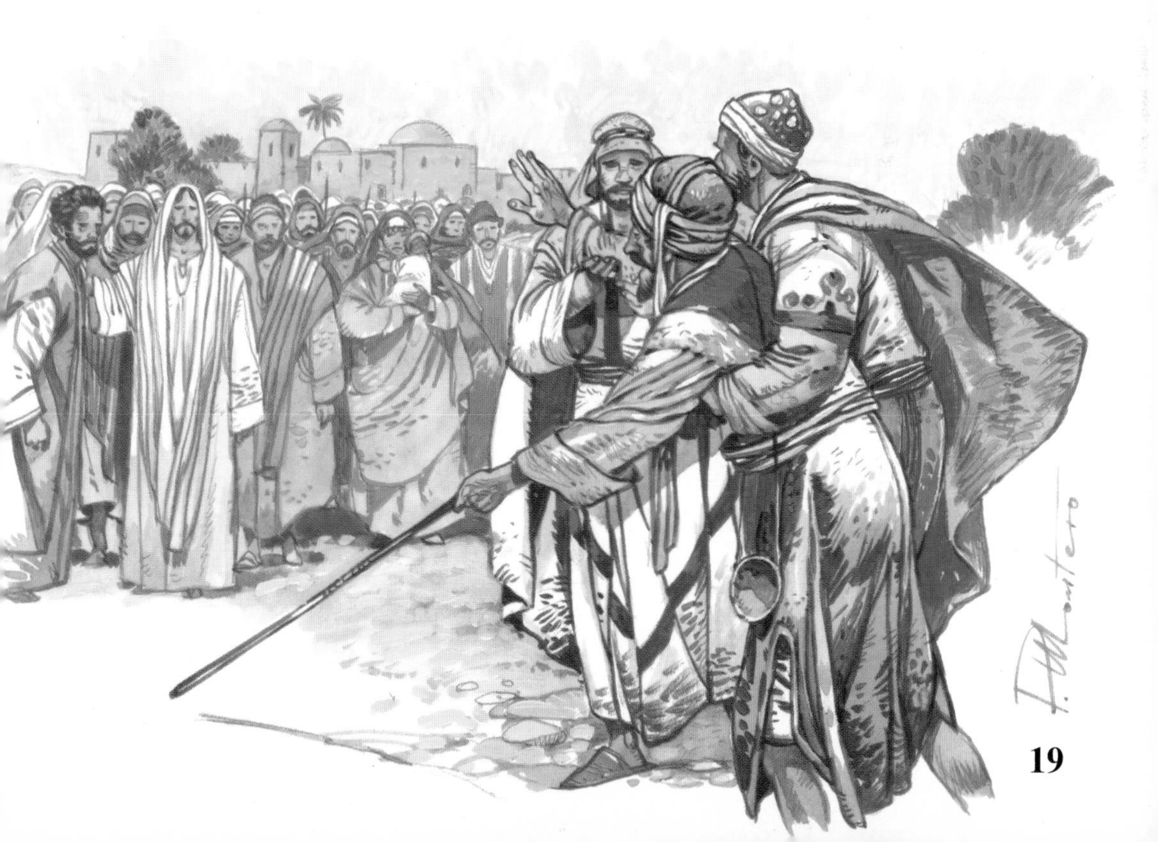

The Man in the Tree

Luke 19:2-10

A man named Zaccheus, a tax collector, was in the crowd that waited for Jesus to pass by as He came into Jericho. But Zaccheus was very short, and could not see over the heads of all the other people. So Zaccheus climbed a tree.

The people below him started cheering. Zaccheus saw Jesus come down the dusty street. Just as Jesus passed beneath Zaccheus' tree, Jesus looked up. Jesus said to him, "Zaccheus, hurry and come down, for today I must stay at your house."

Zaccheus practically fell out of the tree, he was so surprised. He grinned and felt like he wanted to jump for joy. "What an honor!" he thought to himself. He scrambled down the tree and led Jesus toward his home.

But the people they passed on the way grumbled, "Look at that Jesus. There He goes again, staying with sinners."

When Zaccheus had welcomed Jesus to his house, he made a promise. "From now on, Lord, I will give half of whatever I earn to the poor, and I'll give back four times whatever I have stolen from others in the past."

Jesus said, "Today you and your family are saved. That's why the Son of Man has come, to find and save everyone who is lost."

How to Work Hard When No One Is Looking

Luke 19:11-27

Jesus told His disciples this story, knowing that His time on earth was almost over.

"There once was a nobleman who went to a faraway country to be made king. Before he left home, he called ten of his slaves and gave them each the same amount of money. 'Do business with this until I come back,' he told them.

"A long time later, the king came home again. He called the ten slaves and asked how they had used the money he gave them.

"The first slave said, 'Master, the money you gave me has earned ten times as much.'

"'Well done. Now I'll put you in charge of ten cities.'

"Then the king called the second slave. He said, 'The money you gave me has made five times as much.'

"'For this I'll put you in charge of five cities,' the king said.

"But one of the other slaves said, 'Master, I wrapped the money in a cloth and made sure no one stole it.'

"The king was angry. 'Then you will be judged by your own words, you worthless slave! The least you could have done was put the money in the bank so it could earn interest!'

"The king said to the people nearby,

'Take the money away from this man and give it to the one who earned ten times the amount. Those who have something will get more. But the one who does not have, even what he does have shall be taken away.'"

Jesus and the Expensive Perfume

Matthew 26:6-13; Mark 14:3-9; John 12:1-8

The last stop Jesus made before He arrived in Jerusalem was the little town of Bethany. There He surrounded Himself with His best friends, including the twelve chosen disciples, Mary, Martha, and their brother Lazarus. Lazarus was the man Jesus had brought back from the dead.

On this last evening before they entered Jerusalem, Jesus' friends could not help but think He was walking into a trap. The religious leaders in Jerusalem had warned Jesus that they would kill Him the first chance they got.

That night, at dinner, Mary did something very special. She anointed Jesus with costly perfume. It was as if she knew Jesus would be leaving soon.

Mary came into the room, carrying a small jar. The jar contained pure nard, a perfume every Jewish woman saved for her wedding. Mary's perfume was worth as much money as a man could earn in one year.

With tears streaming down her face, Mary poured the ointment on His head and feet. Then she knelt and wiped His feet, with her hair.

The other guests watched silently. No one moved. The rich scent swept through the room, and the house was filled with fragrance. But there were some there who did not like what Mary had done. They thought Mary should have sold the perfume and given the money to the poor.

"Leave her alone," Jesus said. "She has done a beautiful thing to me. You'll always have the poor with you, and you can help them whenever you want. But you won't always have me.

"She did what she could to get my body ready for burial. And I tell you, wherever the gospel is preached, the story of what Mary has done tonight will be told. People will never forget her for this."

PALM SUNDAY

The Big Parade

Matthew 21:1-7; Mark 11:1-7; Luke 19:29-35; John 12:12-16

Jesus led His disciples out of Bethany toward Jerusalem, which was only two miles away.

Many foreigners were in Jerusalem to celebrate the Jewish Passover. All these people heard that Jesus was on His way into the city. They took palm branches and went out to meet Him. Palms stand for victory.

Just outside Jerusalem there was a wooded hillside called the Mount of Olives. When Jesus reached this place, He sent two of His disciples to a nearby village. "Go there, and you will find a donkey's colt that has never been ridden. Bring it to me. If anyone asks what you are doing, say, 'The Lord needs the colt.'"

When the disciples had brought the donkey back to Jesus, they laid their cloaks over the colt and Jesus rode toward Jerusalem. The crowd following Jesus joined the crowd that had come out to meet Him. They began to praise God loudly.

In the past, the people had waved palm branches for kings who had won wars. Now they saw Jesus as their king, one who might deliver them from the Romans.

But Jesus is not that kind of king.

Jerusalem! Jerusalem!

Matthew 21:8-11; Mark 11:8-11; Luke 19:36-44; John 12:17-19

As Jesus came near Jerusalem, the crowd of disciples was shouting, "Hosanna to the Son of David! Blessed is He who comes in the name of the Lord!"

In Jerusalem people asked, "Who is this? What is going on?"

The crowd answered, "This is the prophet Jesus, from Nazareth in Galilee!"

The Pharisees were not happy. "You see," they said to each other, "the whole world is following Him now." They grew especially angry when the people shouted, "Blessed is the King who comes in the name of the Lord!"

Some of the Pharisees said to Jesus, "Tell Your disciples to be quiet."

"If I did that," Jesus said, "the very stones of Jerusalem would shout the same."

Then Jesus looked out over Jerusalem, and tears ran down His face. He was crying for Jerusalem. "If only you could believe what you see today. But you will be blind and your enemies will destroy you, all because you did not recognize and believe!"

Even as the people cheered Him, Jesus knew they would soon betray Him. And He wept for the disaster their wrong choice would bring upon them. He was crying out of love for the very people who soon would scream for His death.

F. Montero

MONDAY

Cleaning Out the Temple

Matthew 21:12; Mark 11:15-16; Luke 19:45

In Jerusalem, Jesus went to the temple. He was not happy with what He saw. Three years earlier, when Jesus was just beginning His public ministry, He had run through the temple, throwing all the loud and greedy people out. But they had come back.

The money changers forced the people, even those who were very poor, to pay high prices for the animals they came to sacrifice at the temple.

Jesus knew this and as He looked around and saw people shouting prices, selling doves and sheep, there was no sign of respect for the place as a house of God.

Jesus overturned the tables of the money changers and those selling doves. Coins splashed onto the ground. People shrieked, running in every direction. Birds escaped their cages and flew frantically out the windows. Jesus went from corner to corner, throwing all the greedy people out.

Healing in the Temple

Matthew 21:13-17; Mark 11:17-18; Luke 19:46-48

Jesus told the money changers and others in the temple, "The Scriptures say, 'My house shall be called a house of prayer,' but you are making it into a robbers' den!"

Now the temple was empty, except for Jesus' followers and a small knot of religious leaders, whispering in the corner.

People who were blind and lame came and asked Jesus to heal them, and He did.

The little children who saw these things began to shout, "Hosanna to the Son of David!"

"Do you hear what they are saying?" the Pharisees asked Jesus. He replied, "Haven't you read the part of Scripture that says that little children and babies will praise God?" The religious leaders grew more intent on killing Jesus. But they couldn't find a way to do it, for all the people were hanging on His words.

TUESDAY AND WEDNESDAY

The Two Sons

Matthew 21:23-32; Mark 11:27-33; Luke 20:1-8

The next day, and the next, Jesus taught in the temple. It was an exciting time, for the city overflowed with people from many lands.

But the more popular Jesus became with the people, the more hatefully the Pharisees plotted against Him. Again and again they tried to trap Him into wrong answers, so they could turn the people against Him.

They asked Him what right He had to preach in God's name. Jesus cleverly turned the question around and asked the Pharisees a question they couldn't answer.

Then Jesus told the Pharisees this story. "There once was a man with two sons. He went to the first and said, 'Son, you go work today in the vineyard.'

"The son said, 'Yes, Father, I will.' But the son did not go and work.

"Then the man went to his second son and asked the same thing. But this son said, 'No, I don't want to work today.' Yet later he changed his mind and went to work anyway.

"Which of the two sons did what his father wanted?" Jesus asked the Pharisees.

"The second son," they said.

Then Jesus said, "The people you call sinners are entering the kingdom of God before you. You did not believe John the Baptist, but they did. And even when you saw them change their lives, you would not change yours."

The Wicked Workers

Matthew 21:33-41; Mark 12:1-9; Luke 20:9-16

Jesus told the Pharisees another story.

"There once was a rich landowner who planted a vineyard. He left his workers in charge while he went away on a trip. When the grapes were ripe, the landowner sent three of his slaves to collect the grapes. But the workers attacked his slaves and beat them up.

"Then the landowner sent a second group of slaves. But they, too, were beaten by the wicked workers. Finally, the landowner thought to himself, 'These people have shown no respect for my slaves. If I send my son to collect the grapes, surely he will be respected.'

"But when the landowner's son arrived at the vineyard, the workers said to each other, 'This is the man who will inherit all this land. If we kill him, we can steal the land.' Then they threw the young man out of the vineyard and killed him."

Jesus asked the Pharisees, "What do you think the owner of the vineyard will do to these workers when he comes?"

The Pharisees answered, "He will bring those wretches to a wretched end and rent out the vineyard to other workers."

Then Jesus asked, "Do you remember the part of Scripture that says, 'The stone the builders did not want became the very foundation. This was from the Lord and is a marvelous thing'?

"The kingdom of God will be taken away from you and given to other people who know how to obey God."

Then the Pharisees gasped, "He's talking about us!" They looked for a way to arrest Him, but they were afraid of all the people.

The King's Son

Matthew 22:1-14

Jesus told this story about the kingdom of Heaven.

A king gave a wedding party for his son. He sent out his slaves with invitations, but no one wanted to come. He sent more servants with invitations, but no one paid any attention and everyone went his own way, one to his farm, another to his business. Some even beat the slaves who brought the invitations.

This made the king very angry. So he sent his armies and destroyed all the people he had invited, setting their city on fire. Then he ordered his slaves, 'The wedding is ready, but those who were invited don't deserve to come. Go stand by the road and invite as many people as you see.'

"Soon the wedding hall was filled with dinner guests—good people and bad people.

"But the king came in and saw one man not wearing the fine clothes that had been given to the guests. 'Isn't my dinner important enough for you to bother changing clothes?' he asked. He ordered the guest to be thrown out and punished."

"In the kingdom of Heaven," Jesus finished, "many are invited, but few are chosen."

Old Testament

P. Montero

Book 16 Slavery—Daniel In Babylon

2 Kings 24, 25; 2 Chronicles 36; Jeremiah 24, 30, 31, 37—40, 46—52; Ezekiel 24—32; Isaiah 13—24, 40—43; Psalm 137; Lamentations; Obadiah; Daniel

Book 17 Freed—The New Jerusalem

Ezekiel 33—37, 40—48; Jeremiah 42—44; Isaiah 44—48; Ezra 1—4; Chronicles 2, 36; Nehemiah 7; Esther

Book 18 Reform—The Last Prophets

Nehemiah 1—10, 12, 13; Ezra 4—10; Haggai; Zechariah; Malachi; Isaiah 56—66

New Testament

Book 19 Gospels—The Early Years of Jesus

Isaiah 9, 11, 12; Luke 1—5; Matthew 1—4; Psalm 139; Micah 5; Mark 1, 6; John 1, 2

Book 20 Miracles—Healing Minds and Bodies

John 2—5; Luke 4—7, 11; Isaiah 53; Mark 1—3, 11; Matthew 5—10, 12

Book 21 Jesus—Following the Messiah

Matthew 8—14; Luke 7—9, 11—13; Mark 3—6

Book 22 Ministry—Jesus Touches People

Matthew 14—18; Mark 6—9; Luke 9; John 6

Book 23 Teaching—The Greatest C

Matthew 18; Luke 9—11, 13—15, 17;

Book 24 Stories—Believing the Tru

Luke 15—20; Matthew 19—22, 26; M

Book 25 Jerusalem—Jesus is Betra

Matthew 22—26; Mark 12—14; Luke

Book 26 Death—Darkness before t

Matthew 26, 27; Mark 14, 15; Luke 2

Book 27 Risen—A New World

Matthew 28; Mark 16; Luke 24; John

Book 28 Acts—The Early Church

Acts 9—19; James; Galatians; 1 and

Book 29 Paul—The First Missiona

1 and 2 Corinthians; Acts 20—28; Ro

Book 30 Christians—Yesterday, T

Philemon; 1 and 2 Peter; 1 and 2 T
Jude; 1, 2 and 3 John; RevelatMion